HAL LEONARD BLUES KEYBOARD METHOD

The Player's Guide to Authentic Stylings

BY MARTY SAMMON
Foreword by Chuck Leavell

To access audio visit:
www.halleonard.com/mylibrary

Enter Code
7513-8862-7416-1276

ISBN 978-1-4803-6235-2

HAL•LEONARD®
CORPORATION
7777 W. BLUEMOUND RD. P.O. BOX 13819 MILWAUKEE, WI 53213

In Australia Contact:
Hal Leonard Australia Pty. Ltd.
4 Lentara Court
Cheltenham, Victoria, 3192 Australia
Email: ausadmin@halleonard.com.au

Visit Hal Leonard Online at
www.halleonard.com

CONTENTS

FOREWORD

My dad used to tell me, "Son, there is an art to everything." That statement has never been truer when it comes to blues piano. It is not easy to play blues piano in an authentic, legitimate style. It is a special skill that needs to be learned, developed, and understood. There is much more to it than you may think. It takes a lot of patience, practice, and experimenting to find the right groove, feel, timing, the right chords, voicings, and the right licks to get it down – and to know when restraint is in order. When playing blues piano or keyboards in a band setting, it is also essential to learn the art of listening to all the other instruments and vocals so that you are contributing properly to the song and complementing the other players.

No one knows all this better than Marty Sammon. Marty has played with the best and he has learned from the best. He has developed his own unique style of blues keyboards and is the perfect authority to share what he has learned with those who wish to reach the same heights in the piano and keyboard blues world that he has. Marty has put it all together in this book, and done it in a manner that it can be easily understood and digested. If you're willing to go through the steps he has laid out and to put your heart and soul into the process, the information here can give you the skills needed to "get there." And getting there can be one of the greatest feelings you'll ever know.

So, my fellow radiators of the eighty-eights, dive into the pages of this Blues Piano Bible and go to work. You'll be glad you did!

–Chuck Leavell

INTRODUCTION

My name is Marty Sammon. Over the years, I've played every type of acoustic and electric piano and organ with every type of blues band, from old school to modern. I started with four years of piano lessons that taught me basic fingering and rhythmic skills, then throughout high school I studied mallet percussion and music theory with a private instructor. Though an inveterate fan of playing ragtime piano, I began playing blues almost by accident – when asked, at age 15, to fill in for Eddie C. Campbell's band. My love and appreciation for the blues has deepened ever since. I've been fortunate to make my living playing with bandleaders ranging from weekend warriors to multiple Grammy Award-winning artists.

There are many languages of the blues and there are many languages of blues keyboard playing. In this compilation of lessons, I'll demonstrate the basic all-around skills you'll need to fit into a blues band setting as a keyboardist. Since it's a large part of my background, I tend to focus more on the piano playing aspect of the blues. However, I will demonstrate organ and electric piano skills as well.

In these pages, you'll learn how to use your listening prowess to assess a situation regarding what to play before jumping in with your first choice. (First choices are not always the best choices!) These lessons will leave you with a larger vocabulary to choose from when you approach different blues band situations. They will also give you the acumen to know when to play and when *not* to play. These skills should give you what it takes to bring together a blues band ensemble that plays with the same precision as bands that use written arrangements.

I encourage you to avoid playing exactly what you hear in these lessons. Instead, use the ideas presented to help develop your own sound and identity. A number of these licks are complicated, so start slowly. Some audio examples are just keyboard, while others have a standard four-piece band. The band examples are there to show you how to play off other instruments, as well as to make the sound more realistic.

The most important element to learning is *listening*. If you listen to these examples, as well as good blues recordings, with open ears and open minds, you'll have success. With the concepts contained in this book, you can develop the skill to play in many blues settings and come across as a seasoned professional. You should also have some tasty and flashy secrets to help you get some house. Enjoy!

BLUES VOCABULARY

Blues players use a vocabulary all their own. We'll employ certain terms throughout this book. Some are what you might hear a bandleader say to set up a tune during a live performance. A good understanding of this vocabulary will help guide you through these lessons as well as through real-life situations.

12 Bar-Blues

The 12-bar blues pattern is built around three chords – the tonic (I), subdominant (IV), and dominant (V) of the key. In C major, these chords are C, F, and G. Often, all three chords are in a dominant 7th (V7) form. Measures 11 and 12 of the form are a turnaround section (see below) leading back to the beginning of the form or leading to an ending in the final Chorus. Here is a 12-bar blues structure in the key of C major:

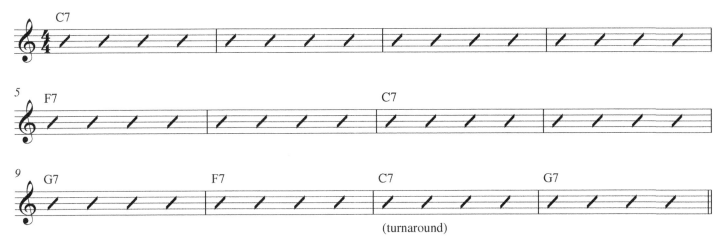

(turnaround)

12-Bar Blues with a Quick Change

Sometimes the chord in measure 2 is replaced by the subdominant (IV) chord. We call this a "quick change."

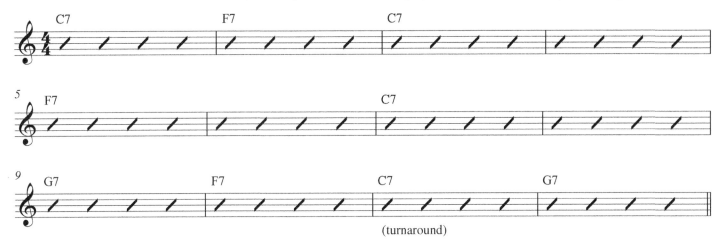

(turnaround)

Turnaround

A "turnaround" is either an ascending or descending phrase during the last two bars of the 12-bar pattern that brings us from the I (tonic) chord to the V (dominant) chord and then back to the I chord that starts the 12-bar pattern over again.

8-Bar Blues

In this eight-bar pattern, there are two bars of the tonic (I) chord, two bars of the subdominant (IV) chord, one bar of the tonic (I) chord, one bar of the dominant (V) chord, then two bars of the turnaround.

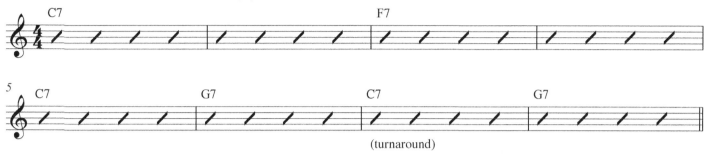

(turnaround)

From the Five (V)

An introduction used before the 12-bar pattern begins, "from the five" contains one bar of the V (dominant) chord, one bar of the IV (subdominant) chord, then a two-bar turnaround.

Come in on the Four (IV)

If a bandleader tells you to "come in on the four," he will play the first four bars by himself; the band begins playing on the IV (subdominant) chord in bar 5 of the 12-bar pattern.

Shuffle

This is a blues rhythmic pattern in which the first and third notes of a triplet are played within each beat. In a blues band setting, the bass and drums set up this feel. Usually, the bass drum plays quarter notes, while the snare and bass player move around; i.e., they "shuffle."

Lump-D-Lump

This is a form of shuffle in which the bass drum and bass player play the first and last note of the triplet. The bass player generally stays on the root note, creating what sounds like "lump-d-lump-d-lump." Both shuffles and lump-d-lumps have the accent on the second and fourth beat of each measure.

Slow Blues

"Slow blues" is a slow, triplet-feel version of the blues pattern. It is sometimes notated in 12/8 time. The upbeat (third note of the triplet) is generally not accented, but the second and fourth "big beats" of the measure are.

Funky Blues

This is a straight-eighths feel within a 12-bar blues pattern. The accents usually occur on the upbeats, creating a syncopated feel called "funk."

Ice Cream Changes

Set in 6/8 time, "Ice Cream Changes" is a pattern commonly found in 1950s era doo-wop recordings. The chord progression is I–vi–ii–V7. It repeats over and over. Each chord change usually takes one bar. The following example is in the key of C major.

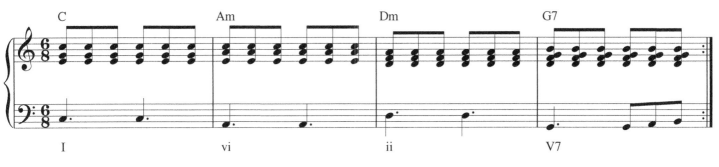

Slop (Grease)

This is a term used to describe exactly what it sounds like. Slop! If we were to play blues very clean and proper, it wouldn't be called blues anymore. While playing two-handed piano, think of two people on each end of a row boat. The person in back is rowing backward, while the person in front is rowing forward. This creates a push-pull effect we call "slop" or "grease."

Get House

By playing something that is special, valuable, or extremely soulful, we elicit a rousing response from the audience. In other words, people are clapping their hands! That's what it means to "get house."

ENSEMBLE PLAYING

Any group of musicians playing music together is considered an ensemble. The key words in that phrase are "playing together." In my local and world travels, I have come across way too many groups of musicians that may be playing the same song, or think they are, but are not necessarily playing it *together*. There's a huge difference.

For example, if a bass player in the group is playing the proper bass line in the proper range, there most likely isn't any need for you as a keyboard player to be playing near his or her range. If a guitarist is comping chords in the middle of the neck, there's no reason for another guitarist or keyboardist to do the same. However, I see this sort of thing happen all the time. And the reason this happens is because the players don't listen to what the others are doing.

What's even sadder is that I see this more in the blues genre of music than any other. I think the reason for this is that many people perceive the blues as an unstructured, sloppy form of music. There are those that consider blues music an uneducated style of music, primarily because of its famous – and some say limiting – three-chord pattern.

However, if you take blues music examples from history and really listen to what's happening, you'll realize that playing blues not only takes a great deal of skill, but it also takes great confidence and trust to play properly as a blues music ensemble. And remember that none of what happens is written out. It occurs spontaneously among the musicians creating the sound.

MAKING CONVERSATION WITH MUSIC

There are two types of conversations I hate ending up in. The first is the kind of conversation where everyone is trying to say the same thing as everyone else – and everyone just gets louder and louder. Second, and even worse, is the sort of conversation where everyone is trying to say something different – at the same time and at the same volume. Everyone has been there. It can be torture!

What's even more annoying is when musicians try to do this with musical instruments. In order to talk with people using a different language, we have to listen to the dialect and timing of how they speak to know when it's okay to contribute something to the conversation. It's the same when playing keyboard in a blues band setting. If you're a sideman keyboard player, meaning that you're not leading the ensemble, it's good to know the person you're playing behind and also to know what their influences are and what their sound is like.

You might find yourself in a situation where you've never met a single person sitting on the stage with you. Let's say you're about to play a blues shuffle in G. At this point, it's a good idea to play just enough to add something at first, until you can figure out where everyone else's mind is. (They're trying to figure you out, too.) Then, add more if needed.

A lucky thing for us keyboard players is that, if we're not the leader, we can get away with more than a bassist or drummer, because – for the most part – we're not relied upon to set the groove or root notes. This is different, of course, if we are acting as the bandleader.

My favorite part of being a sideman keyboard player is participation in "call and response" playing. When performing with Buddy Guy, I often wait for him to play a lick on the guitar. If there's space or if the situation calls for it, I play something on the piano to answer what he said in his playing. Specific examples of this are found in the lessons that follow.

Here's the point I'm making: You should *never ever* get in Buddy Guy's way – or any other bandleader's way – by playing what you feel is superior to what they're trying to express. Having spent over a decade with Buddy, I can easily anticipate when there will be space for me to play. But there are always surprises in this genre of music, too; never let your guard down and always be ready for anything.

Now, it's time to take these ideas and try them out in real-life examples. Remember that this is supposed to be a group effort and, more importantly, it's supposed to be enjoyable. Let's have fun!

INTROS, TURNAROUNDS, LICKS, & ENDINGS

INTRODUCTIONS

There are many ways to begin a blues song, but I have discovered that most of these different intros have many similarities. My goal is to give you enough knowledge to be able to "fall into" whatever situation is thrown at you.

Instead of looking at an intro as just a way to begin a tune, see it as a way of setting up the song's main elements – the tempo, groove, feel, and dynamic. It's a means of preparing the listener for what the tune is trying to say.

Let's start with the most common blues intro in history. If you know Muddy Waters' song "Hoochie Coochie Man," then you've heard the type of intro described here. This is the typical piano part during this blues intro. It's played here in the key of A and it's important to keep an element of "slop" in the right hand, while the left hand stays very consistent.

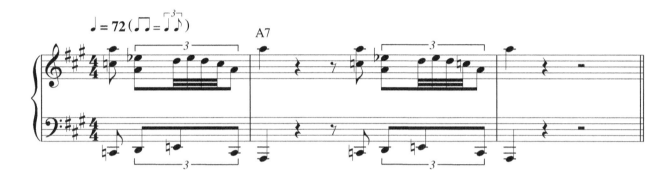

Remember the term "from the five" on page 6? Here's a good idea of what to play on the piano if you're the one who starts the tune that way.

Since we're talking about Muddy Waters, let's play the intro to his famous song "Got My Mojo Workin'" in the key of E, given at the top of page 11. I have heard the same (or a similar) piano intro for other blues songs as well.

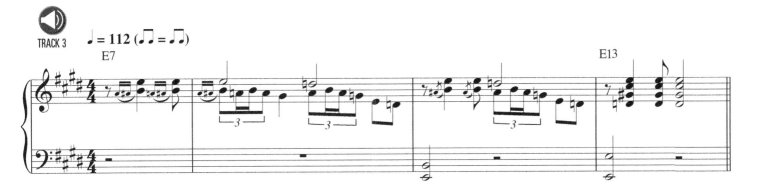

A common way of playing an introduction on the piano for a slow blues song is to begin with a turnaround. Turnarounds are also used at the end of most 12-bar patterns for the duration of a song. Their main purpose is to separate the verses or choruses and set up the next verse or chorus. Here's a common descending turnaround played in the key of G.

Here's a similar descending turnaround, only played an octave higher.

Next is an example of an ascending turnaround.

Here's the same turnaround, only played an octave lower.

Now, let's put one of those turnarounds in the intro and follow through into the I (toni) chord of the 12-bar pattern.

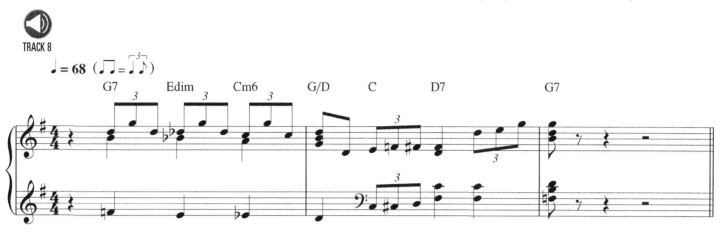

You may wonder why I chose to demonstrate the same example, only an octave lower or higher. The reason is to show how it sets up a different dynamic. Playing a turnaround in the higher octave sets up a more intense feeling for what's coming up next, whereas playing an octave lower prepares a more relaxed feel. This is a key element when playing an introduction. Remember the effect you will have on the other players and the dynamic of the whole ensemble.

Let's now cover a common but very important element in the blues: "call and response." We experience this in the church, in public rallies, in schools, and especially in nature. It basically is what is says – one party makes a call and the second party responds with either the same sound or phrase or a different one.

The famous guitar intro to Elmore James's song "Dust My Broom" is the ultimate example of call and response. On his record, the guitar plays the intro with triplets on a slide. However, the intro lick is used quite often by many different leaders playing different instruments. As a bandleader, I use the guitar part on the piano to kick off a shuffle, like this:

In the example above, the piano is playing the "call" part of the conversation. Next is where the piano plays the "response" part of the conversation by playing in between what the guitar player plays.

Do you hear the "call and response" element to that? Here's another example of what you could play for "response" on the piano.

The following example has the piano playing a bit less and in the lower register. You may encounter a guitar-playing bandleader who wants his instrument to be featured and heard more than the piano. This is what I would play in that situation.

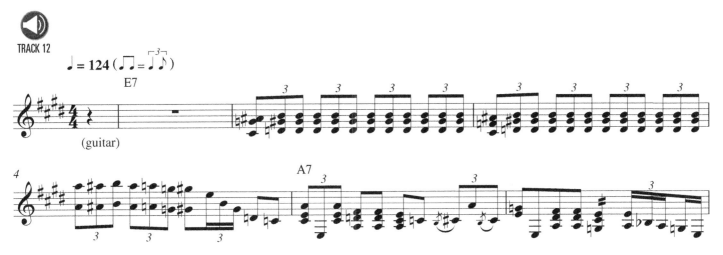

This "call and response" technique can be used in other parts of the song as well; it's not limited just to introductions. It's all a part of the art of conversation and ensemble playing that I keep referring to. Always keep in mind that it's a group effort.

CREATING PIANO SOLOS AND FILLS WITH LICKS

Let's look at some common licks used on the piano during solos or fills. Like I said earlier, don't try to copy these licks verbatim, but use different parts of the examples to form your own tasty solos.

In the key of G, let's use some triplets and an ascending pattern to begin a phrase. This would be a good start to a solo.

In this example, we descend using intervals of a 6th and the "roll" (tremolo) technique.

We can also ascend and descend our intervals or chords. In this next example, the 3rd of the chord is on top.

A "trill" is an ornament that takes two adjacent notes and alternates between them at high speed. Here we have a trill that begins a common lick, similar to "Hoochie Coochie Man."

Here's a lick that incorporates some repetition, in the key of G.

Never hesitate to use the low register, either during solos or while playing behind a singer or soloist. Here is a characteristic Otis Spann type of low-register lick commonly heard on Muddy Waters recordings.

Okay, let's change to the key of F. The next example begins with a tremolo roll and then follows down the blues scale, ending on the root (tonic) note.

Staying in the key of F, we can begin with triplets. What you see in this example is a huge part of my "bag of tricks." It's got it all. Check it out.

In the next example, we play the descending 6th interval that we did earlier in G. Now we're in the key of F. This is a great lick to use at the end of the 12-bar pattern.

Here's a versatile one I use quite often. It begins with the triplet blues scale and can be used as an intro, solo lick, or even an ending in the key of F.

Now we move to the key of A. Guitar players, especially the elders in the blues genre, tend to like to play in the keys of A, G, and E more than other keys. The next example can be used during a solo. However, the more I play and listen to it, the more I tend to use it as an intro.

Like the example above, this pattern can be used as a solo, but I think it makes a wonderful intro. Once again, we're utilizing intervals of a 6th.

I learned some of the following examples from listening to and watching guitar players. B.B. King always said that he tried to play like a saxophone player. When I first started out, I often found my piano solos sounding like guitar solos. That's not a bad thing, because we can use these licks with good keyboard technique to create something different and special.

The next lick is in the key of A. It features a descending chromatic pattern in the beginning.

Now we move to the key of E. Sometimes I like to play licks with a repeated top note and use the bottom notes to invent the melody. This tends to create good tension in a solo.

The next example begins with a bold statement on the root note. Then it incorporates triplets and gets down to the low register. See if you like it as much as I do.

Here's another ascending/descending example with some rolls in the key of E.

To some beginners, the key of C may seem like the easiest key to grasp improvisation on the keyboard. Let's try some soloing in that key. Here are some examples; they each have their challenge. First, we begin with the tonic (I) top note remaining consistent while the bottom note plays the melody. We also roll quite a bit here.

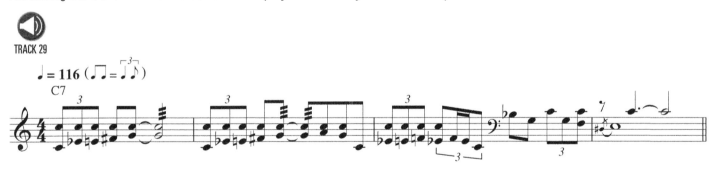

I like to call this next example the "train sound." It opens with a diminished chord that resolves to tonic, followed by a melody in the lower voice as the top note repeats the dominant (V) note, G. Then it descends to resolve once again.

Next, we have what's sort of the opposite of the "train sound." This incorporates sixth intervals while descending in the key of C. Notice how we end on the G. Therefore, we can use this as an intro, or perhaps an ending as well.

TRACK 31

ORGAN LICKS

Let's talk about the organ for a bit. We can use many of the same licks demonstrated on the piano, but simply transfer them to the organ. The attack is very different, but you can use the vibrato and the expression (volume) pedal to create the effect you're going for. I have a few tricks I like to use on the organ that separate my organ playing from my piano playing.

The following is what we call an "organ swell." Take your left hand and use the palm of your hand to sweep up the keyboard to land on a chosen chord. The chord in this example is a G7.

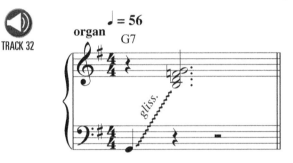

TRACK 32

My favorite trick on the organ is called "chops." In this case, I play a G7♯9 chord and then play triplet chops. The third note of the triplet is simply my left hand hitting a cluster of lower notes, creating a percussive effect.

TRACK 33

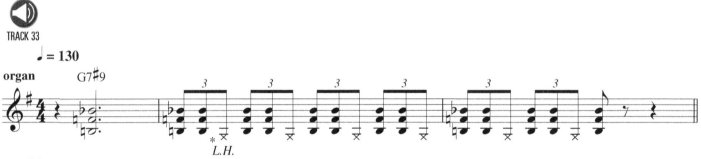

* Left hand plays a cluster of notes.

This lick can also be played on the clavinet. The example is in E minor and it descends, using chord intervals while playing triplet chops.

TRACK 34

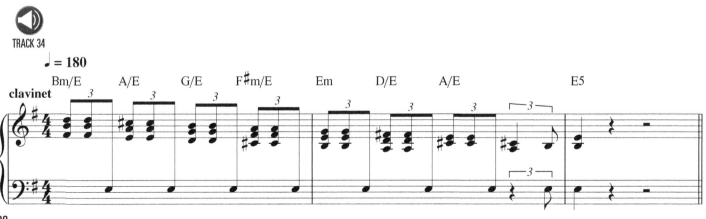

ENDINGS

When it comes time for the song to end, the bandleader will usually cue the band shortly before it's time to stop. On any tune with a blues pattern, the turnaround is usually played, followed by the root chord being held until someone cues the final hit. Sometimes we do a walk-down ending. After the turnaround, we play the II chord, the ♭II chord and then we hold the I chord. This example is played in the key of E.

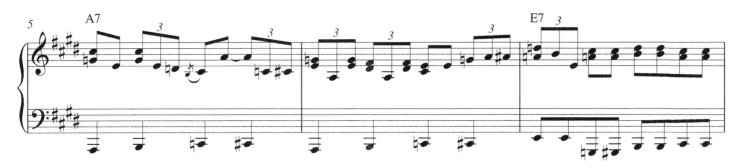

PIANO ACCOMPANIMENT

SHUFFLES

There are many different shuffle patterns you can play on the piano. I call this one the "piano chop." You simply chop the chords of the pattern.

TRACK 36

Another idea is to play a selected riff over the changes, repeating the riff throughout. Here's one you can use on many tunes, including B.B. King's "Rock Me Baby."

TRACK 37

It's important not to be monotonous with your playing. Use the idea of ensemble playing to determine how to change up what you're laying down during a shuffle. In this example, the piano sets up the groove and the bass line by playing the first four bars solo; then the band comes in on the IV chord. The piano plays groove but also interjects some solo-type licks in between.

TRACK 38

(band enters)

During a shuffle with a heavy triplet feel, I may play something similar to what I learned from New Orleans pianist James Booker. This can be played a bit "sloppy" to achieve the "grease" we're looking for. The audio here is just piano so that you can hear the contrast between left hand and right hand.

During a swing shuffle, sometimes it's cool to accent the upbeat and/or double the bass line to create a boogie effect. Instead of going to the V chord for two bars, we can play one measure of the II chord, then one measure of the V chord. Remember: If you're playing in a band setting with a bass player, double the bass part with your left hand only if both are you are playing the same notes. The audio here is just piano so that you can hear how the root notes coincide with the right hand.

SLOW BLUES

To study slow blues accompaniment, let's start with triplets. Playing the chord changes with triplets is a conventional way to accompany a singer or soloist. Place your chord voicings in a register of the keyboard where they don't get in the way of other instruments or the singer. (Note: A "register" is a general area of the keyboard, either high, middle, or low.) Here's an example of solo piano accompaniment with triplets using a "quick change."

TRACK 41

Now let's add the band. Here's an example of playing triplets to back up a guitar solo, similar to a B.B. King feel. I learned this type of playing from B.B. King's legendary album *Live at the Regal*. The slow blues piano on that record is amazing. It's simple and repetitive, but it tickles the listener at exactly the right time. I advise players never to copy a record verbatim, but it's definitely worth listening to and studying. On the next example, the piano changes register occasionally, but it keeps the triplets in the right hand throughout.

TRACK 42

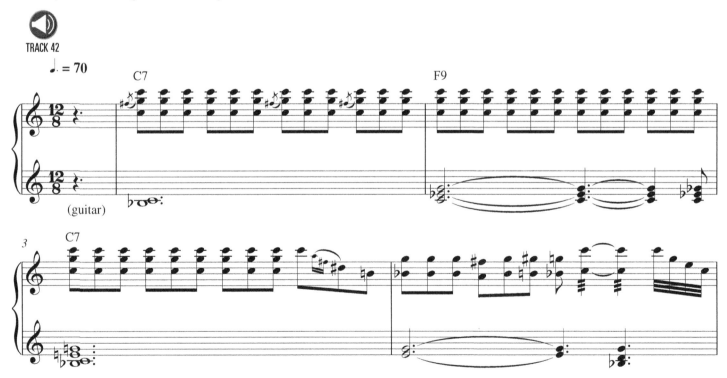

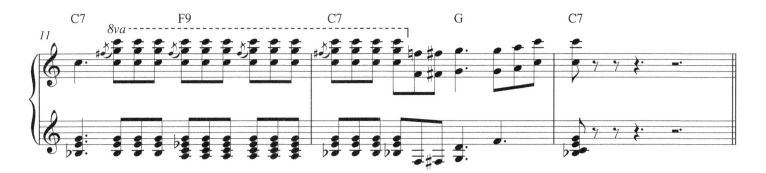

We can stray away from the constant triplets in the right hand and play around what the guitarist is doing. Keep in mind the ideas of "musical conversation" and ensemble playing.

TRACK 43

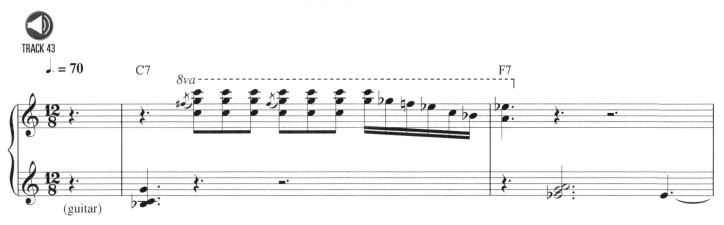

(guitar)

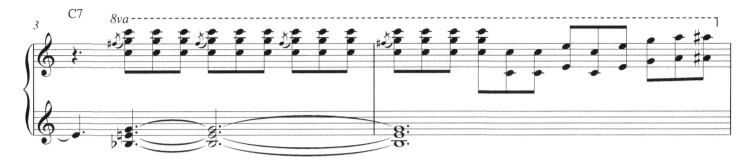

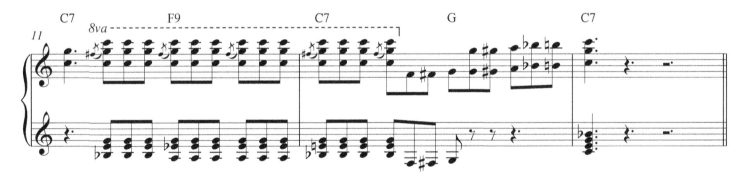

Now let's combine a few skills. The following is a slow blues "from the five." The piano plays triplets, but also adds in some solo-type licks to keep it from becoming monotonous. Notice the typical slow blues band ending.

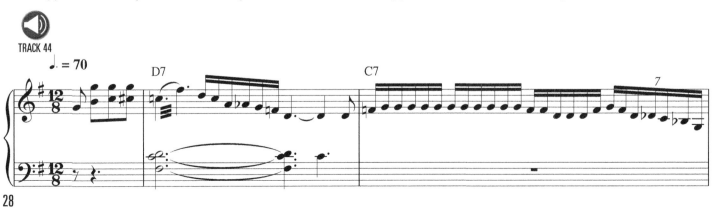

29

We can create a special effect called "tremolo" by rapidly reiterating a note or chord. (We've seen this in a few previous examples.) Playing a tremolo for as long as we please, we can develop a dramatic bed for a soloist to play over. This example presents several ideas about how this effect might be used, and includes a different ending than the last.

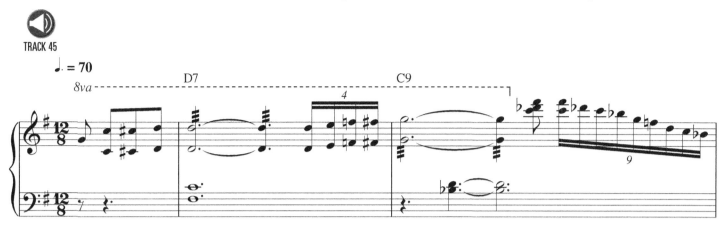

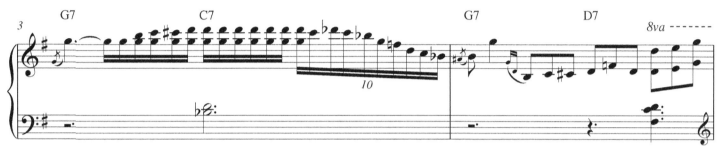

Muddy Waters had a unique way of starting his slow blues with his slide guitar. The piano would play behind what the slide was doing. Although the slide is pretty simple, the piano has a chance to play around the slide and then set up the beginning of the pattern by interjecting a V (dominant) chord with a raised 5th at the end of the turnaround.

TRACK 46 ♩. = 64

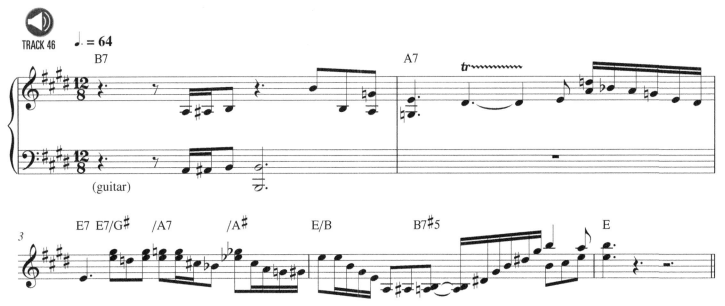

Here's another example of the same basic idea, but with a busier piano part. This is representative of the style of pianist Otis Spann.

♩. = 64

TRACK 47

THE SLIDING LEFT HAND

While playing slow blues, especially something by Muddy Waters that featured Otis Spann on piano, I like to throw in a trick I call "the sliding left hand." I make the transition from the I chord to the IV chord by sliding quickly from the root note of the I (tonic) to the root note of the IV (subdominant).

STRAIGHT-EIGHTH-NOTE BLUES

Playing straight-eighth-note blues isn't that different from shuffles or slow blues. The same concept of accompaniment applies. The groove is different, so there's new vocabulary we can use on the piano. Nothing captures this better than Howlin' Wolf's "Killing Floor." This same bass line and groove are used on other tunes by the Wolf – and other bandleaders as well. It's a common groove to play on jam nights and gigs. Here's an example of what to play.

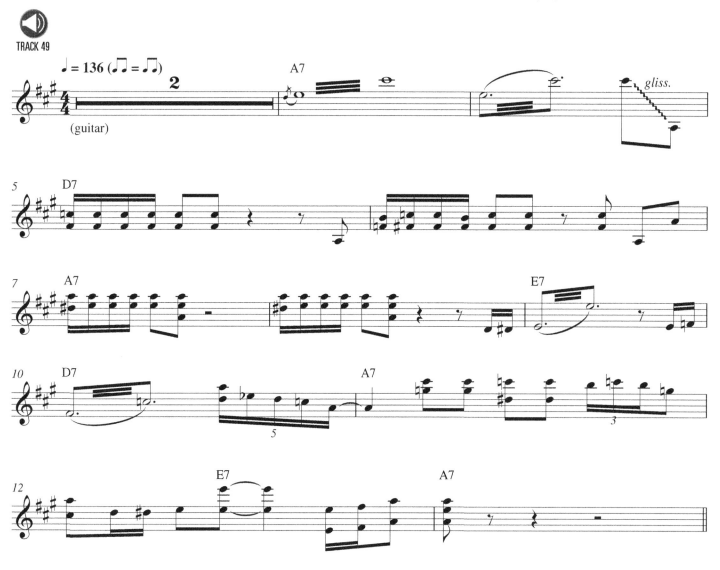

We can change it up and make it busier if we want more intensity.

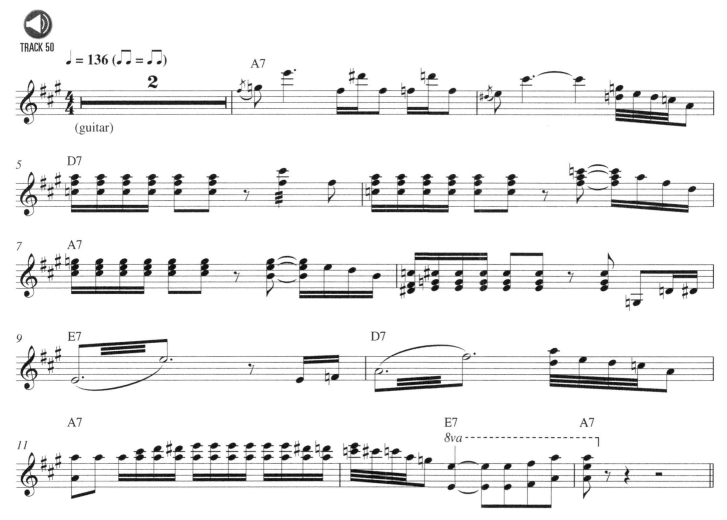

ROADHOUSE BOOGIE

One of my favorite grooves to jam on is what I call a "roadhouse boogie." The next example stays on the I chord in the key of A. It's fun to play because there are no rules or chord changes so we can just jam and play whatever we feel. Keep it a bit sloppy and don't lose the juke joint feel. This example incorporates many of the piano licks demonstrated so far.

RHUMBA

The Rhumba groove is used quite a bit in Chicago blues, but especially in New Orleans blues. It's another fun way of incorporating common piano blues licks with a different rhythm. When performing rhumba, it's important not to play too busily, because the rhythm section is playing its heart out, setting up the groove.

CHICAGO SOUL

Growing up in the Chicago Blues scene, I was thrown into situations where I had no idea what to play. I was lost when bands would play soul tunes. However, I was quickly able to adapt because quite a few of the tunes played on the circuit had simple, repetitive chord changes. Tyrone Davis is one of the pioneers of Chicago soul music and many of his tunes are staples in the Windy City milieu, even today. I tend to use electric piano sounds on tunes like this, but they can be played on the acoustic piano as well. Here's an example of a Tyrone Davis-type of soul tune, with electric piano accompaniment. Note how the keyboard plays chords and lets the guitar player establish the busy part of the groove.

JAMES BROWN FUNKY SOUL

We can't discuss soul without talking about the "Godfather of Soul," James Brown. I don't think I've ever been on a gig or at a jam where we didn't play this James Brown type of groove. It's considered funky because of the syncopation. While playing this style, repetition is a key element. This is where the keyboard truly becomes a percussion instrument. While grooving on the tonic (I) chord, the piano repeats the same thing for as long as the bandleader wants to stay on that chord. Then, when James Brown (or any bandleader) says "Take me to the bridge," we go to the subdominant (IV) chord. This is the spot where we want to open it up a bit and let the chord build up the intensity.

This is a good time to re-introduce the clavinet sound into our playing. (See Track 34.) The clavinet is definitely a percussion instrument. We want to create the funky groove by playing a staccato rhythmic line throughout. This takes incredible discipline not to overplay, change, or lose the groove.

ICE CREAM CHANGES

"Ice Cream Changes," much like 12-Bar Blues, is the basis for countless songs in every genre of music. (See page 7.) Probably the most common way to approach this style of piano accompaniment is simply to play triplets around the chord changes. The next example stays in a decidedly major mode with a frequently heard major ending.

ORGAN ACCOMPANIMENT

Learning how to play the organ in a blues band setting was probably the most difficult element of my career, but it was also one of the most fulfilling. There are a few reasons for this. First of all, I never played a real organ until I started playing with major artists, so I was thrown in with no experience. This turned out to be a good thing, because learning organ technique "on the fly" has opened up my mind on so many levels, musically speaking.

The organ in no way behaves like a piano. Therefore, when I took what I knew about playing the piano and applied it to playing the organ, I found that some of my knowledge was useless. But I didn't give up. I decided to take my piano skills and come up with my own style of organ playing that could be identified easily, while I still performed the musical duties of whatever situation I was in. Let's talk about what it takes to achieve this.

BASIC ORGAN SKILLS

There are several things you need to know to get the most out of what you play on the organ.

First off, the organ is designed with unweighted, waterfall keys. If you use a digital keyboard, keep this in mind. The organ does *not* get louder if you play harder. You need to use a volume pedal to get the dynamics you are looking for.

Also, the organ is fitted with drawbars that represent the size of the pipes on a pipe organ. Note that often there are harmonics on some of these settings that create dissonance. We can use that dissonance to our advantage or, on the other hand, it could get us kicked off the stage. The following audio track is an example of one chord being played while the drawbar settings are changed; the point here is to demonstrate the full potential of the organ.

TRACK 57

Now, let's talk about the rotating speaker. In the blues and church settings, organists use a rotating "Leslie" speaker to create vibrato at their command. The beautiful thing about the Leslie is that there are two rotating speakers inside a wooden cabinet and the high end spins faster than the low end. However, the speed of both of these can be controlled by the player. There's usually a switch between slow and fast vibrato. Track 58 allows you to hear the difference.

TRACK 58

If you're playing organ on a digital keyboard, there are probably different organ patches based on different drawbar settings. Try them all out and be familiar with the sound of each different patch so you can use them accordingly.

CHORD VOICINGS

When thinking about how to voice a chord, especially on the organ, always remember that the two most important notes of any chord are the 3rd and the 7th. In a G7 chord, for example, the two most important notes are B and F. As long as there's a bass player or some other element defining the root note, which in this case is G, this stands true. Keep this in mind while choosing your chord voicings on the organ, because too many notes of the chord on the organ will get in the way of what else is going on. If there's a guitarist playing chords, there's no reason to be playing the same voicing as he is. When in doubt, always revert back to the 3rd and 7th.

Let's begin with what I call "whole-note harmony." I'd like to take credit for this term, but I initially heard it on my first blues gig ever. I was playing with Eddie C. Campbell and, being young and immature, I played as much as possible right out of the gate. He came over and told me, "All I want all night is a whole-note harmony on the organ!" It took me a while to calm down and play just those chord harmonies. But when I finally locked in, I understood my role in creating a unique ensemble sound.

Here's an example of whole-note organ harmony for a shuffle in G.

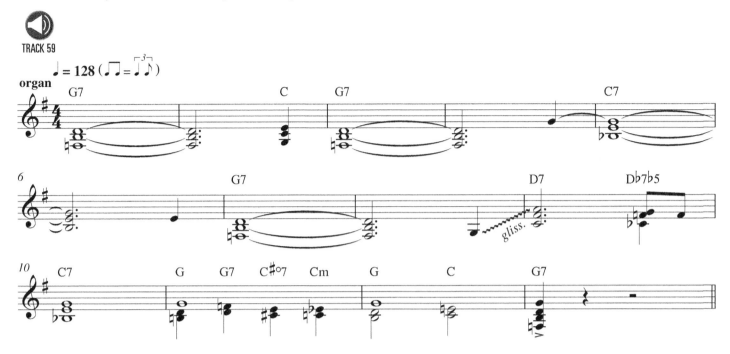

The same concept applies playing a slow blues on the organ. In the following example, the whole note harmony really creates a bed for the guitarist to play over. On the audio track, note the change of Leslie speed for dramatic effect when we get to the V chord.

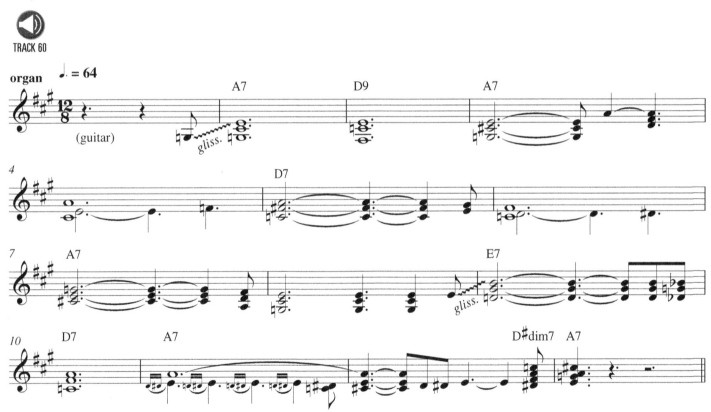

In the course of my career, I've played with artists who like a bit more rhythm from the organ player. To that end, I've learned how to "chop" during a shuffle. This doesn't mean we chop through the whole thing; you'll see some sustained notes in the next example, too, but it's a good illustration of chop accompaniment.

Now let's combine whole-note harmony with the chop effect on a funky minor blues in the key of E minor. Remember to use the chop effect only if it's not getting in the way of another or soloist.

Here's a version of the same E minor blues with a lot more chops, so you can hear the difference.

I spent a huge part of my development listening to legendary blues guitarist Otis Rush and later spent five years as his keyboardist. His most famous tune, "All Your Love," has been covered by blues and rock legends for decades. It's a minor blues rhumba in G minor. This is what I would play over this blues standard or a similar tune with the same pattern.

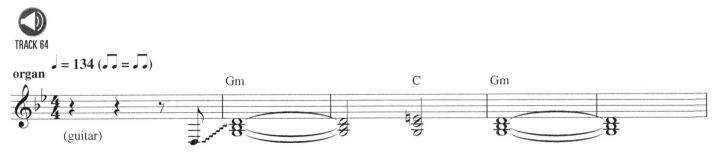

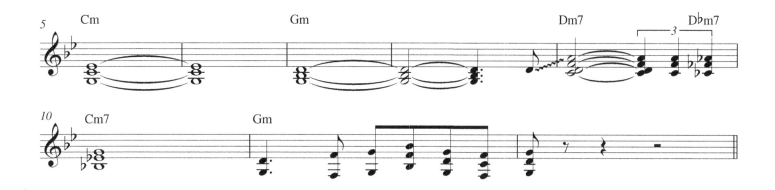

Earlier, we covered Howlin' Wolf and his style. (See page 30.) I love this style because it can be played either on acoustic piano, electric piano, or organ. Here's a combination of chop and whole-note harmony on organ for Howlin' Wolf.

Here's another example of the same tune with much more chop in the organ.

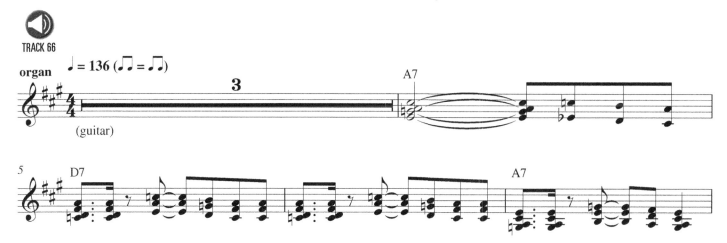

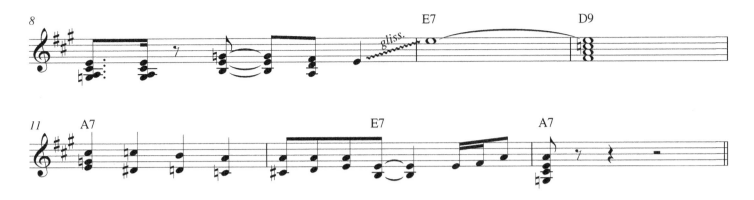

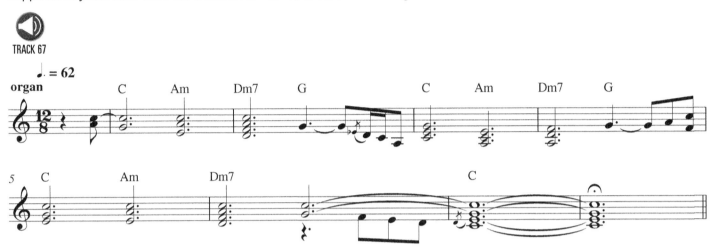

We can use the organ to create real dynamics while playing Ice Cream Changes. I highly recommend playing whole-note harmony during this. I also like to lag a bit between chord changes since the guitar and bass define when the change happens. Keyboardists have the freedom to "dance around" the changes a bit.

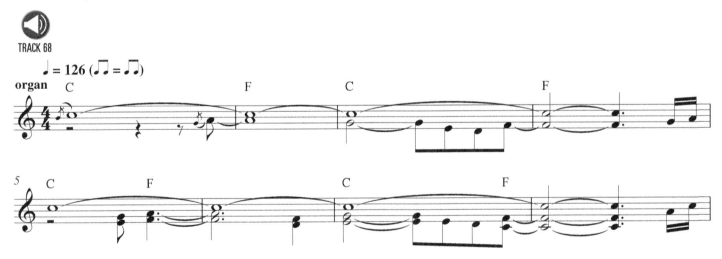

Earlier, we discussed Chicago Soul for the piano. (See page 33.) Track 68 demonstrates what the organ might play on the Tyrone Davis-type example. In reality, if you can play the piano part and the organ part together, it will really fill out the band. However, these individual examples work just as well on their own. Personally, I like to sustain a high note on top while making the changes underneath. For this example, you can think like a horn section.

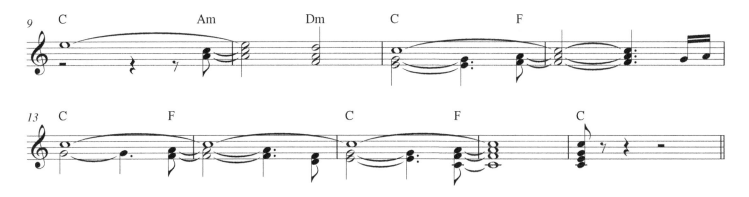

Speaking of horn sections, oftentimes a bandleader will expect the keyboard player to substitute for a horn section. I am not a fan of using horn patches on a keyboard to replace an actual horn sound. Some bands can make that sonority work. However, if you're going to attempt to play a horn section part, it's easily playable on the organ. This B.B. King type of song provides a good example.

Let's take it another step. In many instances, while playing the previous example, someone in the band will cue what we'll call a "triplet climb-up" where we ascend from the I chord to the IV chord chromatically, using triplets. How this happens varies from band to band. Sometimes it's the leader who cues this. Other times, it's the drummer. No matter how it happens in your particular situation, you'd better be ready! Here's how that sounds.

Finally, there's what we call the "Rave-Up." This is what happens at the end of the tune, after the turnaround ending, when the whole band is playing the final chord together. Or it could be used as an intro chord before someone starts the groove. Either way, it's a chance to go crazy and play wild over one chord, with no particular rhythm, just throwing it all out there. Here's one example on organ.

PHRASING AND PLAYING A SOLO

To play a tasteful and impressive keyboard solo, I try to mix the ideas presented in the accompaniment chapters with a variety of keyboard licks demonstrated earlier.

Playing a solo is similar to writing a paragraph. We want to make a point with a beginning, a middle, and an end that finalizes our point. We could take all the licks demonstrated so far and play them in one solo, but that probably would not say anything meaningful.

Remember to use space! There's a time and a place to play something fast, or repetitive, or to "get house" from the audience. But I subscribe to the school of "less is more." Keep in mind the art of ensemble playing and conversation. If we try to converse with someone who never stops talking, it will lead to insanity!

The main element in a great solo is the phrasing. Let's begin with an exercise in phrasing. This example also demonstrates the "blues scale." The blues scale is formulated from the major scale as follows: 1–♭3–4–♭5–5–♭7. Here is the C blues scale

For me, the easiest way to demonstrate this on a keyboard is in the key of F. That's because the key of F is very simple to finger: 1-2-3-1-2-3.

The thumb is the first finger on the right hand. It will move under the third finger on the B♭ to land on the B♮. That's your basic blues scale in F. When I first teach this to students I tell them to play a solo over a blues accompaniment using only these notes in whatever order they please. Feel free to try this.

Now let's take the basic blues scale in F, with the fingering that's given, and use it in a phrasing exercise. Play the scale with the proper fingering, two octaves ascending, then two octaves descending.

TRACK 72

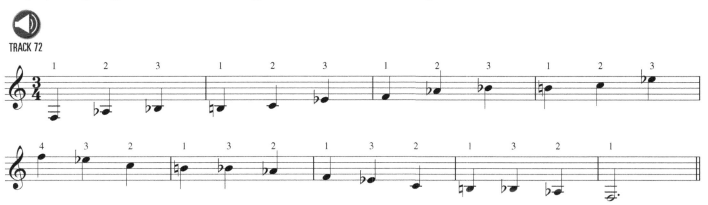

Now, set a metronome to about 72 beats per minute and play this scale as triplets (three notes to each beat). Play two octaves up and two octaves down, like the following example.

TRACK 73

Always keep in mind that when playing blues, funk, or soul music, in a four-beat measure, we want the accent to fall on beats 2 and 4. While playing a solo, we don't necessarily want to accent 2 and 4 constantly, but we want the 2nd and 4th accented beats implied in what we play. Therefore, if we have good phrasing, we should be able to execute a solo with no band accompaniment and still have the listener be able to feel the groove and know where beats 2 and 4 lie.

To achieve this, let's set the metronome at half time and say that it is clicking on the 2nd and 4th beats of the 4/4 measure. Play the triplets like we did earlier, accenting the 2nd and 4th beats where the metronome clicks. This means that we have to know and play the first beat.

Hint: This is easier when the metronome is set at a faster tempo. The slower the tempo, the more space there is between the clicks, leaving more room for error. The more this is done, the less difficult it becomes. I find that this develops great understanding of groove and how to phrase solos around the accents of the groove. This exercise also helps you find the first beat of a groove when it's a song that may be unfamiliar to you, allowing you to "fall into the groove" quite easily.

After we've developed a good groove (or "feel") with the above exercises, we can take the licks we've learned and begin to create solos. Remember that soloing is similar to writing a paragraph, so be sure to make your point. Let's start on piano and a shuffle in the key of A. Here we incorporate the triplet feel, along with ascending and descending intervals of a 6th.

We use some tremolo and some rolls in this solo in A.

Sometimes we can say more with fewer notes. Here's a good example of that, also in the key of A.

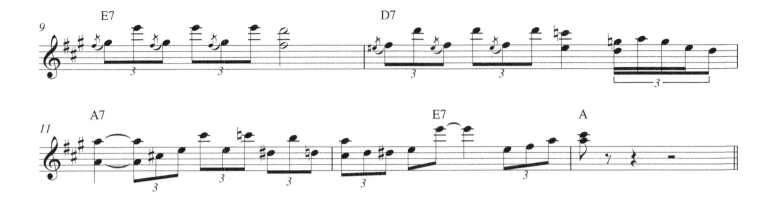

Now let's shuffle in the key of F. The two next examples use licks similar to the ones above; because they are in a different key, however, they create different imagery. Also, I find myself using the fingering shown earlier that makes the key of F so much fun.

This time, let's start out rolling and then do the chromatic descending lick. This is a far more dramatic solo than the last two.

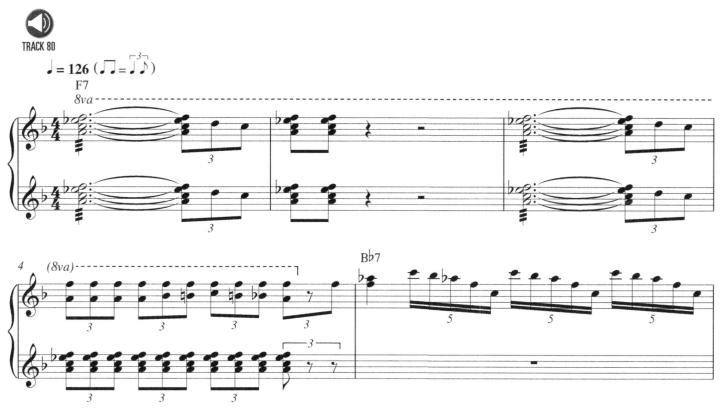

When we solo over minor chord changes, not much is different, except that we need to be aware of the minor 3rd. As stated earlier, if you play a solo with all the right elements, the listener should be able to find the groove and determine the chord changes, even with no accompaniment. Now let's solo over a minor funky blues in E minor. While playing in minor keys, I like to play more melodically so that we keep the dramatic effect of the minor.

Here's an illustration of a repetitive beginning. Toward the end I do some triplet chopping with fully voiced chords.

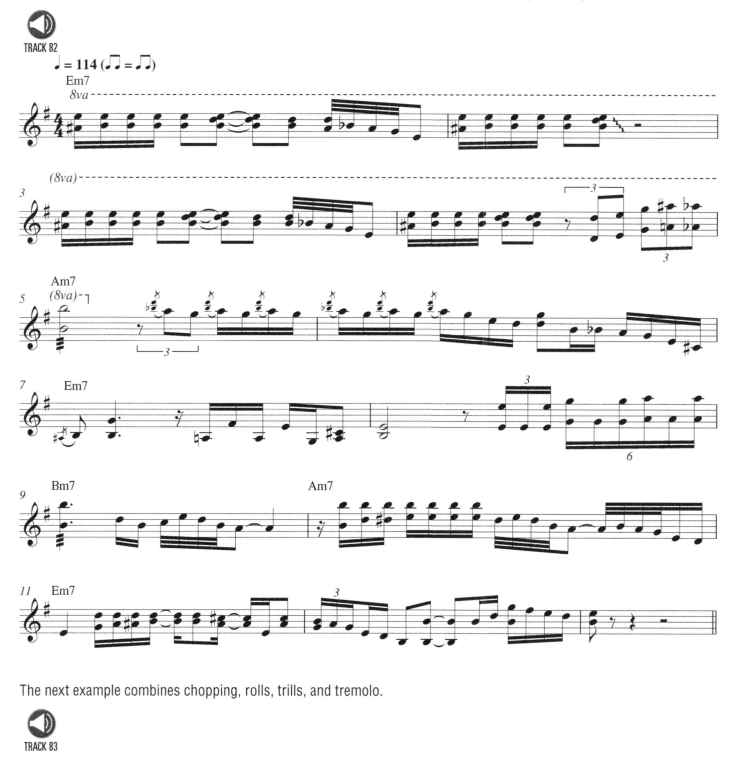

The next example combines chopping, rolls, trills, and tremolo.

We can use the same techniques on the minor blues, but this time using the organ. The chop effect works well on the funky blues style.

Here's a sample with more chops.

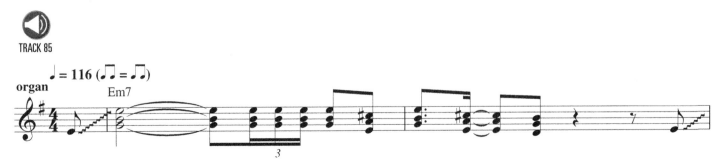

Try this much simpler organ solo over an E minor funky blues.

When we solo over slow blues, we have a bit more room for "slop." That doesn't mean we can be sloppy throughout the whole solo, but we can grease it up a bit more. Be aware that the slower the tempo, the more room there is for mistakes and bad phrasing to stand out.

The following slow blues solo example begins with an introduction and also includes a traditional slow blues ending. It's in the key of G.

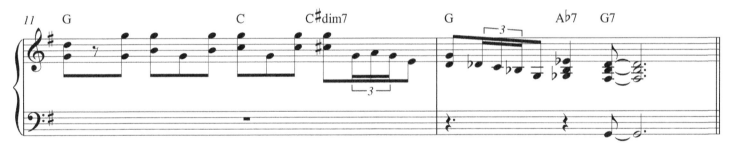

This example tends to show an Otis Spann influence, especially when it takes us down to the low register of the piano.

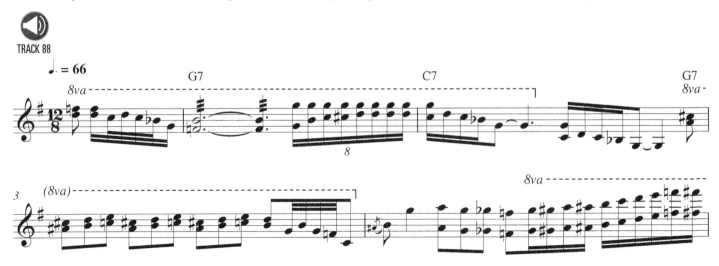

Here I play very melodically, almost like this was the main melody of the tune. This is a good time to make a point: Certain songs have a melody that is so important, it's a good idea to incorporate the melody into your solo. This one is in the key of G.

TRACK 89

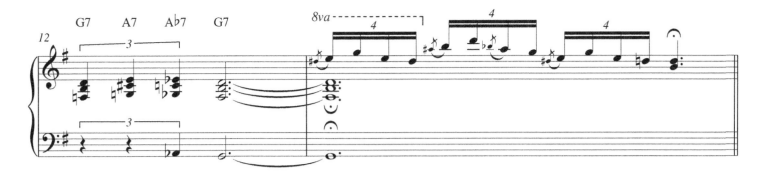

Next are a few slow blues patterns on the organ. Let's play in the key of A. The first includes a lot of whole notes and is rather simple and sustained. This also includes the song ending.

TRACK 90

Here's a melodic specimen with a mellow drawbar setting. This one is jazzier than the others.

TRACK 91

Now let's go full out dramatic! I really like the triplets repeating the same note in the middle of this one. This technique usually helps get house!

ESSENTIAL LISTENING FOR BLUES KEYBOARDISTS

As I tell every student that comes to me looking to improve their blues keyboard playing, listening is the best way to learn the style. Many students come to me looking to learn blues and when I ask them what songs they listen to or like, they are unable to cite a single one!

They expect me or an instructional book to teach them. The thing is, private instructors and method books are excellent tools, but you cannot learn to play blues without listening to blues recordings. Good blues keyboard recordings complete the toolbox. The following are some that I recommend.

B. B. King – Live at the Regal
This was recommended by Buddy Guy, especially because of the pianist and the way he played behind B.B.'s singing and playing.

Muddy Waters – Live at Newport
This is an essential record for your collection, along with any other Muddy record with Otis Spann on piano.

Muddy Water – Hard Again
This is high-energy Chicago blues with Pinetop Perkins on piano and special guest Johnny Winter on slide guitar and screams.

Buddy Guy – The Complete Chess Recordings
This is a great mixture of early Buddy recordings. I'm especially a fan of the piano on some of his slow blues and shuffles.

Albert Collins – Live 92/93
Allen Batts was the keyboardist on this legendary live record that was a huge early influence on me.

Stevie Ray Vaughan – In Step
Reese Wynans really contributes to what was a power trio before he joined the band. There's killer organ from Reese on this record.

Otis Spann's Chicago Blues
This shows all the Chicago piano chops you need to play traditional style!

Professor Longhair – Crawfish Fiesta
Producer Bruce Iglauer captured a unique recording of this New Orleans piano legend that was released before Longhair's death. It's so much fun and there's an incredible amount of piano education here.

Dr. John – Live and Trippin'
This stayed in my cassette player for probably a whole year. It's New Orleans all the way, but it sure shaped my playing big time!

Buddy Guy – Live at Legends
I mention this record to show an example of my playing with the blues legend in a live situation. This is where all of my influences come together. I'm very proud and honored to be featured on this recording.

CONCLUSION

Now that you've played through all the examples and followed the text, you should have enough knowledge to go out and play. And that's my final advice to you all: Play!

In every town or city I've been to, there's always a blues jam night happening at least one night of the week. I strongly believe this is a tradition that will never die.

I also believe that, even though blues music has been called a dying art form, it will be around forever because it's a huge part of our American heritage.

Don't be afraid to sit in with players you've never met. In fact, I urge you to do that. The best way to improve is to put yourself in situations that you are not comfortable in. Before you know it, you'll feel right at home and you'll be amazed at how your playing has improved.

I'm grateful that you've taken the time to study my lessons and I hope that this has been a fun, fulfilling experience.

ACKNOWLEDGMENTS

Marty Sammon's special thanks go to:

- Jeff Schroedl for his input, musicianship, and most of all, his patience
- Bruce Iglauer of Alligator Records
- Phil Summers at On the One Management
- Pete Galanis at 3011 Studios for the great sound
- Lordy at www.chicagobluesbeat.com
- Ted Lemen, Buddy Guy, and the Damn Right Blues Band and crew
- Jonny Lang and his band members and crew
- Giles, Marvin, and Rick for their priceless input and friendship
- Michael Maxson, Garry Buck, and Tom Hambridge

ABOUT THE RECORDING

The audio was recorded at 3011 Studios, Chicago, IL
Engineer: Pete Galanis

All keyboards: Marty Sammon
Guitar: Giles Corey
Bass: Marvin Little
Drums: Rick King

Marty Sammon plays Yamaha Keyboards and Merida Guitars.

For more information, visit:
www.halleonard.com
www.martysammon.com
www.bluesfling.com

ABOUT THE AUTHOR

Photo by Bradley Cook

Marty Sammon was born and raised on the south side of Chicago. His encouraging family and Irish culture provided a solid structure for Marty to demonstrate himself as a musical prodigy. Marty's natural ability and sincere persona were welcomed into a city that is selective to those musicians proven to be aesthetically true to its signature sound. By age 15, Marty was performing with L.V. Banks and absorbing the sonorities and lifestyle of the Chicago blues scene. Shortly thereafter, fate and opportunity collided when Marty's talent earned the attention of Buddy Guy's younger brother Phil.

Phil Guy exposed Marty to a funkier, heavier, more soulful side of the blues, an expression Marty could easily translate. James Montgomery of the Chicago Playboys took immediate notice and introduced Marty to Otis Rush. Marty shared the stage with Otis Rush for five years until he received the call to tour the world and perform with blues legend and Rock and Roll Hall of Fame inductee Buddy Guy. For almost a decade, Marty has been a member of the Damn Right Blues Band and has contributed as a studio musician on Buddy Guy's most recent recordings.

TESTIMONIALS

Marty Sammon is an extremely talented and gifted keyboard player. Whether it's a live situation or in the studio, Marty brings it. He is well-versed in all styles of music and puts a great deal of passion into his craft. Marty has incredible chops, but always puts the song first. He is not only a true professional, but a caring person; this comes across in his playing. I have used Marty on several records and for countless shows. He is a joy to work with.

–Tom Hambridge, Grammy Award-winning producer

I first met Marty through my late brother Phil Guy. The first time I heard Marty perform, he was playing like some of the old New Orleans and Chicago players. He's one of the best I've seen and one of the greatest guys you'd ever want to work with. I'd recommend him to anyone.

–Buddy Guy, Six-time Grammy Award-winning blues artist

Marty Sammon is one of the most legit blues piano players around today. Hearing him, you can tell he has a special understanding of the great, legendary piano players of the genre and ties that knowledge in with his own innovative, unique style. The fact that for years Buddy Guy has felt comfortable with Marty sitting at his right hand every night speaks for itself.

–Jonny Lang, Grammy-Award-winning singer, songwriter, and guitarist

It is a rare opportunity to glean musical insight from someone who is both a passionate player and an invested teacher. Marty is nothing short of a veteran musician, seasoned with stories and wisdom from the road and studio. He offers a treasure chest of experience and fun in his playing, and whoever absorbs his techniques will develop the skills only the masters achieve.

–Dwan Hill, producer, songwriter, keyboardist (Jonny Lang Band)

PLAY PIANO LIKE A PRO!

AMATING PHRASING – KEYBOARD
50 Ways to Improve Your Improvisational Skills
by Debbie Denke

Amazing Phrasing is for any keyboard player interested in learning how to improvise and how to improve their creative phrasing. This method is divided into three parts: melody, harmony, and rhythm & style. The online audio contains 44 full-band demos for listening, as well as many play-along examples so you can practice improvising over various musical styles and progressions.

00842030 Book/Online Audio.. $16.99

BEBOP LICKS FOR PIANO
A Dictionary of Melodic Ideas for Improvisation
by Les Wise

Written for the musician who is interested in acquiring a firm foundation for playing jazz, this unique book/audio pack presents over 800 licks. By building up a vocabulary of these licks, players can connect them together in endless possibilities to form larger phrases and complete solos. The book includes piano notation, and the online audio contains helpful note-for-note demos of every lick.

00311854 Book/Online Audio.. $17.99

BOOGIE WOOGIE FOR BEGINNERS
by Frank Paparelli

A short easy method for learning to play boogie woogie, designed for the beginner and average pianist. Includes: exercises for developing left-hand bass • 25 popular boogie woogie bass patterns • arrangements of "Down the Road a Piece" and "Answer to the Prayer" by well-known pianists • a glossary of musical terms for dynamics, tempo and style.

00120517 .... $10.99

HAL LEONARD JAZZ PIANO METHOD
by Mark Davis

This is a comprehensive and easy-to-use guide designed for anyone interested in playing jazz piano – from the complete novice just learning the basics to the more advanced player who wishes to enhance their keyboard vocabulary. The accompanying audio includes demonstrations of all the examples in the book! Topics include essential theory, chords and voicings, improvisation ideas, structure and forms, scales and modes, rhythm basics, interpreting a lead sheet, playing solos, and much more!

00131102 Book/Online Audio.. $19.99

INTROS, ENDINGS & TURNAROUNDS FOR KEYBOARD
Essential Phrases for Swing, Latin, Jazz Waltz, and Blues Styles
by John Valerio

Learn the intros, endings and turnarounds that all of the pros know and use! This new keyboard instruction book by John Valerio covers swing styles, ballads, Latin tunes, jazz waltzes, blues, major and minor keys, vamps and pedal tones, and more.

00290525 .... $12.99

JAZZ PIANO TECHNIQUE
Exercises, Etudes & Ideas for Building Chops
by John Valerio

This one-of-a-kind book applies traditional technique exercises to specific jazz piano needs. Topics include: scales (major, minor, chromatic, pentatonic, etc.), arpeggios (triads, seventh chords, upper structures), finger independence exercises (static position, held notes, Hanon exercises), parallel interval scales and exercises (thirds, fourths, tritones, fifths, sixths, octaves), and more! The online audio includes 45 recorded examples.

00312059 Book/Online Audio.. $19.99

JAZZ PIANO VOICINGS
An Essential Resource for Aspiring Jazz Musicians
by Rob Mullins

The jazz idiom can often appear mysterious and difficult for musicians who were trained to play other types of music. Long-time performer and educator Rob Mullins helps players enter the jazz world by providing voicings that will help the player develop skills in the jazz genre and start sounding professional right away – without years of study! Includes a "Numeric Voicing Chart," chord indexes in all 12 keys, info about what range of the instrument you can play chords in, and a beginning approach to bass lines.

00310914 .... $19.99

OSCAR PETERSON – JAZZ EXERCISES, MINUETS, ETUDES & PIECES FOR PIANO

Legendary jazz pianist Oscar Peterson has long been devoted to the education of piano students. In this book he offers dozens of pieces designed to empower the student, whether novice or classically trained, with the technique needed to become an accomplished jazz pianist.

00311225 .... $14.99

PIANO AEROBICS
by Wayne Hawkins

Piano Aerobics is a set of exercises that introduces students to many popular styles of music, including jazz, salsa, swing, rock, blues, new age, gospel, stride, and bossa nova. In addition, there is a online audio with accompaniment tracks featuring professional musicians playing in those styles.

00311863 Book/Online Audio $19.99

PIANO FITNESS
A Complete Workout
by Mark Harrison

This book will give you a thorough technical workout, while having fun at the same time! The accompanying online audio allows you to play along with a rhythm section as you practice your scales, arpeggios, and chords in all keys. Instead of avoiding technique exercises because they seem too tedious or difficult, you'll look forward to playing them. Various voicings and rhythmic settings, which are extremely useful in a variety of pop and jazz styles, are also introduced.

00311995 Book/Online Audio.. $19.99

HAL•LEONARD®
7777 W. BLUEMOUND RD. P.O. BOX 13819
MILWAUKEE, WISCONSIN 53213

www.halleonard.com

Prices, contents, and availability subject to change without notice.

0519
057